TABLE OF CONTENTS

Mission

Ensure the regulated entities operate in a safe and sound manner so that they serve as a reliable source of liquidity and funding for housing finance and community investment.

Vision

A reliable, stable, and liquid housing finance system.

FHFA's Values

Respect   We strive to act with respect for each other, share information and resources, work together in teams, and collaborate to solve problems.

Excellence   We aspire to excel in every aspect of our work and to seek better ways to accomplish our mission and goals.

Integrity   We are committed to the highest ethical and professional standards to inspire trust and confidence in our work.

Diversity   We seek to promote diversity in our employment and business practices and those of our regulated entities.

ABOUT THE FEDERAL HOUSING FINANCE AGENCY

The Federal Housing Finance Agency (FHFA) was established by the Housing and Economic Recovery Act of 2008 (HERA) and is responsible for the effective supervision, regulation, and housing mission oversight of the Federal National Mortgage Association (Fannie Mae), the Federal Home Loan Mortgage Corporation (Freddie Mac), and the Federal Home Loan Bank System, which includes 12 Federal Home Loan Banks (FHLBanks) and the Office of Finance. The agency's mission is to ensure that these regulated entities operate in a safe and sound manner so that they serve as a reliable source of liquidity and funding for housing finance and community investment. Since 2008, FHFA has also served as conservator of Fannie Mae and Freddie Mac (together, the Enterprises).

FHFA's Regulatory Oversight of the Federal Home Loan Banks, Fannie Mae, and Freddie Mac. As part of the agency's statutory authority in overseeing the Federal Home Loan Bank System (FHLBank System) and the Enterprises, the Federal Housing Enterprises Financial Safety and Soundness Act (the Safety and Soundness Act), as amended by HERA, requires FHFA to fulfill the following duties:

"(A) to oversee the prudential operations of each regulated entity; and

"(B) to ensure that--

> (i) each regulated entity operates in a safe and sound manner, including maintenance of adequate capital and internal controls;

> (ii) the operations and activities of each regulated entity foster liquid, efficient, competitive, and resilient national housing finance markets (including activities relating to mortgages on housing for low- and moderate-income families involving a reasonable economic return that may be less than the return earned on other activities);

> (iii) each regulated entity complies with this chapter and the rules, regulations, guidelines, and orders issued under this chapter and the authorizing statutes;

> (iv) each regulated entity carries out its statutory mission only through activities that are authorized under and consistent with this chapter and the authorizing statutes; and

> (v) the activities of each regulated entity and the manner in which such regulated entity is operated are consistent with the public interest."

12 U.S.C. § 4513(a)(1).

FHFA's Role as Conservator of Fannie Mae and Freddie Mac. As part of HERA, Congress granted the Director of FHFA the discretionary authority to appoint FHFA as conservator or receiver of Fannie Mae, Freddie Mac, or any of the Federal Home Loan Banks, upon determining that specified criteria had been met. On September 6, 2008, FHFA exercised this authority and placed Fannie Mae and Freddie Mac into conservatorships. Since they were placed into conservatorships, Fannie Mae and Freddie Mac together have received $187.5 billion in taxpayer support under the Senior Preferred Stock Purchase Agreements (PSPA) executed with the U.S. Department of the Treasury. FHFA continues to oversee these conservatorships.

FHFA's authority as both conservator and regulator of the Enterprises is based upon statutory mandates enacted by Congress, which include the following conservatorship authorities granted by HERA:

> "(D) …take such action as may be--
>
> > (i) necessary to put the regulated entity in a sound and solvent condition; and
> >
> > (ii) appropriate to carry on the business of the regulated entity and preserve and conserve the assets and property of the regulated entity."
>
> 12 U.S.C. § 4617(b)(2)(D).

Carrying on the business of the Enterprises in conservatorships also incorporates the above-referenced responsibilities that are enumerated in 12 U.S.C. § 4513(a)(1). Additionally, under the Emergency Economic Stabilization Act of 2008 (EESA), FHFA has a statutory responsibility in its capacity as conservator to "implement a plan that seeks to maximize assistance for homeowners and use its authority to encourage the servicers of the underlying mortgages, and considering net present value to the taxpayer, to take advantage of…available programs to minimize foreclosures." 12 U.S.C. § 5220(b)(1).

FHFA, acting as conservator and regulator, must follow the mandates assigned to it by statute and the missions assigned to the Enterprises by their charters until such time as Congress revises those mandates and missions.

STRATEGIC GOAL 1: ENSURE SAFE AND SOUND REGULATED ENTITIES

As regulator of the FHLBank System and regulator and conservator of the Enterprises, FHFA will promote safe and sound operations at the regulated entities through the agency's supervisory program. FHFA uses a risk-based approach to conducting supervisory examinations, which prioritizes examination activities based on the risk a given practice poses to a regulated entity's safe and sound operation or its compliance with applicable laws and regulations. FHFA conducts on-site examinations at the regulated entities, ongoing risk analysis, and off-site review and surveillance. FHFA communicates supervisory standards to the regulated entities, establishes expectations for strong risk management, identifies risks, and requires remediation of identified deficiencies.

Performance Goal 1.1: Assess the safety and soundness of regulated entity operations

FHFA will assess the safe and sound operations of the regulated entities through annual examinations, targeted examinations, ongoing monitoring, and off-site review, as appropriate. FHFA uses a uniform examination rating system known as CAMELSO to assign ratings for the FHLBanks, the Office of Finance, and the Enterprises. FHFA assigns two ratings: 1) the composite rating for the overall condition of each regulated entity; and 2) the individual component ratings for Capital, Asset Quality, Management, Earnings, Liquidity, Sensitivity to Market Risk, and Operational Risk. FHFA assigns these ratings for each regulated entity on an annual basis.

Performance Goal 1.2: Identify risks to the regulated entities and set expectations for strong risk management

FHFA's supervisory activities will identify existing and emerging risks to the regulated entities. FHFA develops risk assessments by collecting and analyzing information from various sources, including the regulated entities, and coordinates with other supervisory agencies in this process.

In order to articulate supervisory expectations for risk management across all risk types, FHFA publishes guidance for examiners and management at the regulated entities. This includes issuing Advisory Bulletins on specified topics. Additionally, FHFA supervisory guidelines are included in the agency's Examination Manual, which FHFA will revise as necessary. FHFA also issues additional examination instructions to address emerging issues and provide procedural updates.

Performance Goal 1.3: Require timely remediation of risk management weaknesses

In order to assess both timeliness and effectiveness, FHFA will evaluate actions taken by the regulated entities to remediate identified weaknesses. Examination findings and conclusions are carefully documented and communicated to the regulated entities. Where examination staff identify issues that should be addressed, FHFA uses supervisory communications to direct the entity to improve its risk management and address the weakness. FHFA uses three categories of examination findings: 1) Matters Requiring Attention (MRAs), 2) Violations, and 3) Recommendations. MRAs and violations require the regulated entity to take remedial action. Recommendations identify policies, procedures, or practices that could be improved. FHFA subsequently evaluates the actions taken in response to these supervisory communications through its ongoing supervisory work.

Strategic Goal 1—Means and Strategies

- **Conduct risk-based, on-site examination work in accordance with examination plans for each regulated entity, including annual examinations, targeted examinations, ongoing monitoring of particular business operations or programs, and periodic special and horizontal reviews.** FHFA examiners use a risk-based approach designed to: 1) identify existing and potential risks that could adversely affect the regulated entity, 2) evaluate the effectiveness of each entity's risk management and internal controls, and 3) assess compliance with laws and regulations.

  FHFA develops examination plans for each regulated entity that provide tailored on-site examinations based on the agency's risk assessment. In addition to annual examinations, FHFA's supervisory engagement with the regulated entities may include ongoing monitoring and targeted examinations, as well as communication in various formats. FHFA examines risk management practices and the regulated entity's financial condition and safety and soundness relative to applicable laws, regulations, supervisory guidance, and prudent business practice. On-site examinations are a critical means of evaluating the effectiveness of risk management by the regulated entities.

- **Identify Matters Requiring Attention of the regulated entities, assess remediation plans, and monitor remediation for both timeliness and efficacy.** Through its supervisory program, FHFA will identify control weaknesses or other issues that could compromise safe and sound operations. Such weaknesses can result in FHFA issuing an MRA, which reflect the most serious supervisory matters.

  FHFA will communicate examination findings, recommendations, and required corrective action to the regulated entity's management and board of directors. FHFA examiners will obtain a commitment from the management and the board to correct weaknesses or deficiencies in a timely manner and will monitor remediation and verify the effectiveness of corrective actions, as appropriate.

  When deficiencies are severe, or the regulated entity is resistant to remediation, FHFA will pursue an enforcement action in accordance with published policy on supervisory enforcement.

- **Monitor emerging risks, industry trends, supervisory standards, and macro-economic market conditions in order to inform risk assessments and adjust supervisory strategies when appropriate.** The regulated entities operate in markets that are subject to uncertainty, volatility, and changing processes and practices. In order to inform the agency's risk assessments, FHFA will review and analyze relevant data, monitor changing market conditions and developments, and continue to collaborate with other financial institution regulators, where appropriate.

- **Issue regulations, supervisory policies and supervisory guidance in order to set standards and supervisory expectations for safe and sound operation of the regulated entities.** Taking into account examination findings and any analysis of existing and emerging risks, FHFA will issue guidance to examiners and public bulletins to the regulated entities that set forth supervisory expectations in particular areas of risk management, internal controls, or compliance. FHFA will issue and revise regulations and guidance as necessary to ensure the regulated entities' policies and practices on asset acquisition, pricing, investments, and other matters are consistent with safe and sound practices.

- **Strengthen training and development of examination staff.** FHFA will enhance examiner capability through the ongoing development and administration of examiner education and accreditation programs. FHFA will also continue to develop technical training on market developments, emerging risks, FHFA guidance, and sound industry practices and standards.

- **Perform off-site analyses of key risk areas to strengthen supervision.** Off-site analyses of key risk areas complement on-site examinations by bringing cross-disciplinary resources that support FHFA's risk-based approach to supervision. Off-site analyses are based upon reviews of data reported by the regulated entities, published financial statements and reports, other available sources of data on housing finance trends, and market drivers of financial results, such as interest rates, rate spreads, and house prices.

  Off-site analyses address issues such as financial market conditions, the effect of changes in interest rates and house prices on the financial condition and risk exposure of the regulated entities, management of troubled real estate assets, and executive compensation. FHFA will continue ongoing off-site monitoring of financial trends and emerging risks of the regulated entities.

STRATEGIC GOAL 2: ENSURE LIQUIDITY, STABILITY, AND ACCESS IN HOUSING FINANCE

Performance Goal 2.1: Ensure liquidity in mortgage markets

For both the FHLBank System and the Enterprises, FHFA has the statutory obligation to enable "liquid, efficient, competitive, and resilient national housing finance markets" while ensuring that the regulated entities meet their fundamental safety and soundness obligations. FHFA's responsibilities of housing finance market liquidity and safety and soundness are inherently intertwined. FHFA will evaluate policies and take appropriate action to promote both goals.

Federal Home Loan Banks: The FHLBanks' core mission is to serve as a reliable source of liquidity for their member institutions in support of housing finance and community lending. As regulator of the FHLBank System under the Safety and Soundness Act and the Federal Home Loan Bank Act, FHFA will work to ensure that the FHLBanks continue to fulfill their statutory mission of providing liquidity to their members.

The Enterprises: As both regulator and conservator of the Enterprises, FHFA will require the Enterprises, where feasible, to: (i) take actions to improve liquidity in the present single-family housing finance market, (ii) continue to improve servicing standards and foreclosure prevention actions, and (iii) have a critical ongoing role in the multifamily sector, particularly for affordable multifamily properties and underserved market segments.

Performance Goal 2.2: Promote stability in the nation's housing finance markets

FHFA will focus on promoting stability in housing markets, both as regulator of the FHLBank System and regulator and conservator of the Enterprises. In support of this objective, FHFA will seek to provide clarity and certainty about the agency's supervision and conservatorship expectations of the regulated entities. In addition to seeking feedback from the regulated entities, FHFA will seek public input from market participants and stakeholders on priority issues. FHFA will also provide notice, as appropriate, when significant policy decisions require market implementation. Additionally, FHFA expects the regulated entities to promote stability in the nation's housing finance markets by establishing transparent and well-reasoned policies and procedures.

As conservator of the Enterprises, FHFA will also promote stability by working to preserve and conserve the Enterprises' assets and business operations. Additionally, FHFA will encourage the Enterprises and the housing industry to adopt standards and practices that stabilize housing markets and promote market and stakeholder confidence.

Performance Goal 2.3: Expand access to housing finance for qualified financial institutions of all sizes and in all geographic locations and for qualified borrowers

Having a housing finance market that provides liquidity throughout the country requires strong participation by a wide range of lenders, including small lenders, lenders serving rural areas, and state and local Housing Finance Agencies. Additionally, a healthy housing market requires liquidity and access across different borrower market segments to provide homeownership opportunities to creditworthy borrowers, sensible and appropriate loss mitigation options when borrowers fall into economic distress, and affordable rental housing options. However, even in liquid markets and especially during times of market uncertainty, some qualified borrowers and financial institutions may face barriers and disruption in their access to financing. FHFA is committed to ensuring that qualified financial institutions and creditworthy eligible borrowers have fair and equitable access to the financial services offered by the regulated entities.

Strategic Goal 2—Means and Strategies

- **Promote actions by the Enterprises to maintain liquidity in the single-family secondary market for purchase money and refinance mortgages.** FHFA will continue to focus on meeting the goals of the conservatorships by maintaining their support for the housing finance market and mitigating losses to taxpayers. FHFA will work to ensure ongoing liquidity in the marketplace for new mortgages and mortgage refinancings and continue the critical tasks of foreclosure prevention and loss mitigation.

- **Promote actions by the FHLBanks to maintain sufficient liquidity by providing advances in a safe and sound manner.** FHFA will work to ensure that the FHLBanks can continue to provide advances in a safe and sound manner. FHFA will examine the FHLBanks' operations, internal controls, and strategic assumptions and evaluate whether there are unnecessary impediments to their ability to efficiently and competitively provide liquidity to members through normal or stressed markets and during expansion and contraction cycles.

- **Monitor access to mortgage credit.** FHFA will assess trends in the availability of mortgage credit to both single-family and multifamily borrowers. FHFA will monitor access to mortgage credit using data reported by the regulated entities, data from third-party sources, and discussions with industry sources. FHFA's assessment of access to mortgage credit will inform potential policy initiatives.

- **Support multifamily housing needs with a focus on the affordable and underserved segments of the market.** The Enterprises play a significant role in supporting multifamily housing needs, particularly for low-income households. FHFA expects the Enterprises to maintain a multifamily liquidity presence in all geographic areas and through all market cycles with a focus on the affordable segment of the market. In instances when FHFA imposes a production cap on the Enterprises' multifamily business as part of the annual conservatorship scorecard, FHFA will not count certain mission-related activities – such as affordable rental housing, buildings with 50 or fewer units and manufactured rental housing communities – toward the production cap in order to encourage purchases in these underserved market segments.

- **Collaborate with other federal regulators to identify and address risk and other emerging issues.** FHFA works with other federal regulators through its participation on the Financial Stability Oversight Council, the Financial Stability Oversight Board, the Federal Housing Finance Oversight Board, and other interagency initiatives. FHFA will continue to collaborate with other regulators to identify and address foreign and domestic risks, to coordinate supervision efforts consistent with each agency's respective examination and supervision responsibilities, to complete interagency rulemakings, and to pursue efforts that streamline and increase efficiency of regulatory activities.

- **Monitor housing markets and conduct independent studies and reports.** FHFA will continue to develop a series of studies and reports that analyze various factors impacting access to housing finance for qualified borrowers and financial institutions. The information resulting from this analysis will contribute to FHFA's ability to ensure liquidity, stability, and access in the housing finance markets. Additionally, FHFA will continue to develop monthly and quarterly house price indexes reflecting changes in house prices in each of the states and nine Census divisions.

- **Develop and actively promote home retention and loss mitigation programs.** Home retention initiatives, such as loan modification and refinancing programs, help reduce the number of defaults and foreclosures by allowing eligible borrowers to realize more favorable rates or terms on their mortgages. Such initiatives reduce losses to the Enterprises and contribute to greater stability and liquidity in housing markets and neighborhoods.

While FHFA has established a solid foundation for servicing standards and loss mitigation efforts, more work can be done to address particular issues and better target these efforts. FHFA expects the Enterprises to make further progress on refining and improving their servicing standards and loss mitigation outcomes. This includes supporting the following priorities:

o Build upon the Servicing Alignment Initiative to develop consistent standards for the Enterprises for resolving delinquencies, including long-term loss mitigation standards after the conclusion of the Home Affordable Modification Program;

o Target outreach for the Home Affordable Refinance Program (HARP) in order to reach the markets with the highest incidence of borrowers who would benefit from HARP refinancing; and

o Continue the Neighborhood Stabilization Initiative to target loss mitigation efforts to communities hardest hit by the ongoing foreclosure crisis to help stabilize local markets, provide targeted assistance to eligible homeowners, and mitigate credit losses to the Enterprises.

- **Promote policies and practices at the regulated entities to provide fair and equal access to finance and financial services for all eligible financial institutions and qualified borrowers.** FHFA will work with the FHLBank System to ensure that FHLBank membership and advance policies permit fair and equal participation by eligible institutions. FHFA will also work with the Enterprises to address barriers for small lenders, lenders serving rural areas, and state and local Housing Finance Agencies.

  Consistent with the safety and soundness of the Enterprises, FHFA is committed to reducing barriers that restrict creditworthy borrowers' access to responsible lending. FHFA will continue to work with the Enterprises, lenders, and other stakeholders to provide greater clarity regarding both origination and servicing obligations. Greater certainty regarding both origination and servicing obligations should help increase lenders' willingness to more fully provide credit within the Enterprises' underwriting standards. FHFA also expects the Enterprises to assess whether there are additional opportunities to reach underserved creditworthy borrowers.

- **Promote and ensure diversity and inclusion of minorities and women in the business and activities of FHFA and the regulated entities.** The Safety and Soundness Act and the Dodd-Frank Wall Street Reform and Consumer Protection Act require FHFA, Fannie Mae, Freddie Mac, and the FHLBanks to promote diversity and inclusion of women and minorities in all activities. FHFA will provide technical assistance to, and oversight of, the regulated entities in their supplier diversity, board diversity, and workforce diversity compliance activities. This will include developing innovative initiatives to expand outreach to advance inclusive access and participation in all aspects of the business activities of the agency, the Enterprises, the FHLBanks, and the Office of Finance.

- **Oversee the Regulated Entities' Additional Statutory Requirements.** FHFA will meet its statutory responsibilities to issue regulations as needed defining the regulated entities' Housing Goals and the Duty to Serve standards for the Enterprises. FHFA will also continue to monitor and examine the FHLBanks' activities under the Affordable Housing Program (AHP) and Community Investment Program (CIP).

STRATEGIC GOAL 3: MANAGE THE ENTERPRISES' ONGOING CONSERVATORSHIPS

Performance Goal 3.1: Preserve and conserve assets

FHFA's authority as both conservator and regulator of the Enterprises is based upon statutory mandates enacted by Congress to ensure a liquid, efficient, competitive, and resilient national housing finance market, ensure safe and sound Enterprise operations, as well as to preserve and conserve their assets. FHFA will oversee the conservatorships of the Enterprises in their current state and seek to ensure that the Enterprises' infrastructures meet the needs of their current credit guarantee businesses and other operations. FHFA will also maintain programs and strategies to ensure ongoing mortgage credit availability, assist troubled homeowners, and minimize taxpayer losses. While the Enterprises are in conservatorship, FHFA will strive to maintain core business operations, maintain executive management and board oversight, ensure timely replacement of departing senior executive officers and board members, and provide clear expectations to Enterprise boards and management.

FHFA will develop an annual Conservatorship Scorecard to guide Enterprise management in fulfilling FHFA's *2014 Strategic Plan for the Conservatorships of Fannie Mae and Freddie Mac* and will establish performance metrics to measure how well the Enterprises are meeting their Scorecard goals.

FHFA will oversee the Enterprises' adherence to the Senior Preferred Stock Purchase Agreements and will work with the Administration and the Enterprises to reduce borrower defaults, encourage home retention by borrowers, and minimize losses to the Enterprises.

Performance Goal 3.2: Reduce taxpayer risk from Enterprise operations

FHFA is focused on ways to bring additional private capital into the housing finance system to lessen taxpayer risk by reducing Fannie Mae and Freddie Mac's overall portfolio risk exposure. FHFA's objective is to shift risk to private market participants and away from the Enterprises in a responsible way that does not reduce liquidity or adversely impact the availability of mortgage credit.

This priority includes having the Enterprises conduct additional credit risk transfers for their single-family credit guarantee business. The transactions to date have attracted private capital to share in credit losses, which protects taxpayers from bearing all of the potential losses. FHFA is also overseeing ongoing and required reductions in the Enterprises' retained portfolios. The Senior Preferred Stock Purchase Agreements with the U.S. Department of the Treasury require the Enterprises to reduce their portfolios to no more than $250 billion each by 2018. FHFA is requiring that the Enterprises prioritize selling their less liquid portfolio assets and develop plans to meet the PSPA 2018 portfolio reduction goals even under adverse market conditions. Another risk-reduction priority involves private mortgage insurer counterparties. The work FHFA is undertaking will strengthen master policies and eligibility requirements for private mortgage insurers, a critical source of private capital in the mortgage finance markets.

Performance Goal 3.3: Build a new single-family securitization infrastructure

Building a new infrastructure for the securitization functions of the Enterprises remains an important priority for FHFA. This includes ongoing work to develop the Common Securitization Platform (CSP) infrastructure and to improve the liquidity of Enterprise securities. Additionally, FHFA continues to work to build more accurate and uniform mortgage data standards used by both the Enterprises and other market participants.

Ongoing development of the CSP will focus on making the new shared system operational for existing Enterprise single-family securitization activities. Developing this shared infrastructure will require modifying the Enterprises' current securitization systems, software, and processes so that they can effectively integrate with the CSP. Targeting the CSP development to the Enterprises' current functions will allow FHFA and the Enterprises to manage appropriately the risk of launching this new joint venture. While FHFA will require the Enterprises to build the new infrastructure for use by both companies, FHFA will also require that the CSP be adaptable for use by additional market participants in the future. As a result, the Enterprises and CSP team will continue to focus on leveraging industry-standard interfaces, industry software, and industry data standards where possible.

In order to leverage CSP advantages fully, FHFA is also prioritizing ways to improve the overall liquidity of the Enterprises' securities. This includes working toward the development of a Single Security, which should reduce the trading value disparities between Fannie Mae and Freddie Mac securities. The different mortgage securities currently issued by the Enterprises are not fungible with one another, and Freddie Mac's security has historically traded less favorably compared with Fannie Mae's security. As part of the effort to create a Single Security, FHFA and the Enterprises will define parameters for a Single Security, including security characteristics and disclosure requirements.

FHFA continues to oversee the Enterprises' activities to provide active support for mortgage data standardization initiatives. Developing and implementing mortgage data standards is essential to improving accuracy, increasing transparency, effectively assessing risk and pricing, and creating efficiencies for the Enterprises and mortgage industry participants. Improved data collection in the earliest stages of the mortgage process will help the Enterprises identify potential problems and improve the quality of the mortgages they purchase. Current areas of focus include loan application data and mortgage closing data.

Strategic Goal 3—Means and Strategies

- **Provide clear conservatorship expectations to Enterprise boards and management.** FHFA will convey conservatorship restrictions and expectations to the Enterprise boards and management teams to guide the boards and management in carrying out day-to-day operations and setting business objectives.

- **Oversee Enterprise staffing.** Successful accomplishment of FHFA's conservatorship objectives requires qualified boards, CEOs, management and staff at each Enterprise. FHFA will continue to oversee the hiring and retention of boards and CEOs, and through the boards and CEOs, qualified management and staff.

- **Address outstanding claims involving FHFA, Fannie Mae, and Freddie Mac.** FHFA will continue its litigation concerning pre-conservatorship violations of federal securities laws in mortgage-backed securities (MBS) sales to Fannie Mae and Freddie Mac. FHFA has settled the majority of this litigation but several cases remain. FHFA will also continue to monitor any legal developments that might impact FHFA's role as conservator of the Enterprises.

- **Promote credit risk transfers that reduce taxpayer risk by attracting private capital.** FHFA will continue to oversee the Enterprises' activities to increase and deepen credit risk-sharing transactions, setting targets for multiple types of single-family mortgage credit risk-sharing transactions and holding Enterprise management accountable for meeting those targets. FHFA will require that the Enterprises assess the economics and feasibility of additional types of risk transfer structures. FHFA also expects the Enterprises to explore whether transfers of additional risk can be achieved within the Enterprises' multifamily business models by evaluating whether private capital is willing to share additional credit risk for multifamily mortgages and at what cost.

- **Reduce counterparty risk by strengthening master policies and setting appropriate eligibility requirements for Enterprise private mortgage insurer counterparties.** Informed by feedback from relevant regulatory authorities, stakeholders, and industry members, FHFA will continue to guide Enterprise efforts to ensure that their mortgage insurer counterparties are able to provide adequate credit loss protection in times of market stress.

- **Reduce the Enterprises' legacy retained portfolios.** FHFA will continue to oversee the Enterprises' activities to reduce their retained portfolios in accordance with the PSPAs, even under adverse market conditions, focusing on reducing less liquid assets and ensuring that any sales are economically sensible transactions that consider impacts to the market and neighborhood stability.

- **Support the development of a common securitization platform.** FHFA will continue to work with the Enterprises to build a CSP to replace the current separate proprietary systems at each Enterprise. In pursuing this multiyear process, the agency will target development of the CSP to the Enterprises' current functions in order to appropriately manage the risk of launching this new joint venture. When this process is completed in the future, the platform will bundle mortgages into securities structures and will process and track payments from borrowers through to investors.

- **Work toward a Single Security for Fannie Mae and Freddie Mac.** FHFA is in the early stages of a multiyear process to develop a Single Security for securitizations of Enterprise purchased loans. When this process is completed in the future, a Single Security should improve the overall liquidity of the Enterprises' securities. As part of the effort to create a Single Security, FHFA and the Enterprises will define parameters, including security characteristics and disclosure requirements. Throughout this process, FHFA will solicit feedback from the Enterprises and from stakeholder groups.

- **Oversee the Enterprises' implementation of the Uniform Mortgage Data Program.** FHFA will continue to guide Enterprise work on developing uniform standards for mortgage-related data reporting. The Uniform Mortgage Data Program is currently focused on improving the reporting consistency, quality, and uniformity of data collected during the mortgage process in loan application and closing data.

CRITICAL FACTORS THAT AFFECT ACHIEVEMENT OF STRATEGIC GOALS

FHFA faces a series of economic and environmental factors that could influence the agency's success in achieving its goals and objectives. Fragility in domestic and global economies and uncertainty over the future of housing finance reform initiatives affect the financial condition, performance, and future prospects of the regulated entities. FHFA has to meet its conservatorship and supervisory responsibilities for the Enterprises and supervisory responsibilities for the FHLBanks against this backdrop of uncertain economic and environmental factors.

Global Markets

Several external factors in global markets have influenced U.S. markets in the recent past and may continue to affect them in the future. Economic conditions and government policies in foreign markets may affect the pricing of U.S. Government debt and the benchmarks used to price private debt. Solvency concerns in interbank markets could affect the availability of counterparties. External regulatory policies may also affect the Enterprises and the FHLBanks.

The Domestic Housing Market

In past recessions, the housing sector served as a stimulus for economic recovery. Housing production would increase as pent-up demand was released and consumers took advantage of lower interest rates. Housing production stimulated wholesale and retail trades, generated employment, and boosted the financial sector and real estate services. By contrast, the housing market has not led the recovery from the most recent financial crisis and recession. Continued distress sales, fears of future decline in house prices, and homebuyers' concerns about the vitality and sustainability of the economic recovery may limit future gains or reverse recent gains in house prices. Furthermore, tightening of credit standards has reduced the pool of potential buyers, and recent reductions in the share of purchases by first-time homebuyers may be linked to the growing levels of unsecured consumer debt (especially education loans) held by young adults. It is expected that the multifamily market will continue to enjoy strong property fundamentals, growth, and financial performance.

Economic Conditions and the Regulated Entities

The financial condition and performance of the Enterprises and the FHLBanks are dependent on the performance of the U.S. housing and mortgage markets, as well as general business and economic conditions. The Enterprises and the FHLBanks are exposed to credit risk on mortgage loans and mortgage securities held in their investment portfolios. In addition, the Enterprises are exposed to credit risk on mortgage loans that back MBS guaranteed by the Enterprises. Increases in delinquencies, default rates, and loss severity on mortgages and mortgage-related assets could cause further write-downs of investment securities and could lead to an increase in credit-related expenses. The FHLBanks are exposed to credit risk on mortgage loans and securities held as collateral for their advances to members.

Cyclical and structural changes in the competitive landscape in recent years have adversely affected the FHLBanks' primary business of making advances to their members. Since October 2008, the FHLBanks experienced a sharp decline in the demand for advances. The demand for advances has been hurt by a weak economy, resulting in decreased loan demand, and by members' access to alternative funding sources, including an increase in deposits from members' customers. In 2012, the level of advances stabilized, but advances in mid-2014 were approximately 47 percent below their 2008 peak. Domestic and international changes to bank supervision principles have the potential to adversely affect the demand for advances.

Although they have a positive effect on funding costs, low interest rates have dampened revenues from interest-earning assets held by the regulated entities. Meanwhile, continued access to debt markets at attractive rates remains critical to their effectiveness and ability to support housing finance.

The Conservatorships of Fannie Mae and Freddie Mac

The Enterprises were placed into conservatorships in September 2008, in the midst of a severe financial crisis and have been an important factor in the continued operation of the housing finance market. As conservator, FHFA establishes restrictions and expectations for the Enterprises' boards and management, but does not manage day-to-day operations. At the time of the conservatorship, FHFA made the judgment to replace the boards and key senior management at each Enterprise and delegate to the new boards and management day-to-day responsibility for overseeing operations. Since being placed in conservatorships, the reconstituted boards of directors have worked with FHFA to define the operational goals in conservatorship and to complement FHFA's work to guide and oversee management in fulfilling these goals.

As detailed earlier, FHFA's authority as both regulator and conservator of the Enterprises is based upon statutory mandates enacted by Congress. FHFA, acting as regulator and conservator, must follow the mandates assigned to it by statute and the missions assigned to the Enterprises by their charters until such time as Congress revises those mandates and missions. The priorities outlined here in *FHFA's Strategic Plan: Fiscal Years 2015 – 2019* also reflect the strategic goals established in the *2014 Strategic Plan for the Conservatorships of Fannie Mae and Freddie Mac*.

⬛H⬛⬛ Resources

Managing FHFA's resources successfully is critical to goal and mission achievement and will remain an important issue for FHFA over the next four years. Strategic goals and expected outcomes cannot be achieved without prudent and effective management of resources to ensure that the right people, funds, supplies, physical space, and technology are in place. In addition, achievement of FHFA's goals requires communication, collaboration, and coordination by all staff and across all offices and divisions within FHFA.

Responsive, secure, and efficient information technology capabilities are essential to FHFA's ability to accomplish its mission. To meet the information technology demands, FHFA must provide expertise, capabilities, and services in systems development and support. The agency must also meet the needs for data, information, and knowledge management; information sharing; telecommunications and network support; and technical support and security.

FHFA will continue to invest in its human capital by offering a wide array of competency-based learning events, leadership development programs, and organizational effectiveness services that maximize cost efficiencies. The infrastructure of the learning function will continue to mature and deliver necessary knowledge, skills, and development to the FHFA workforce.

FHFA will continue its investments in family-friendly programs, including flexible work hours and other benefits. FHFA will also employ strategies that involve staff at all levels across the agency in achieving its goals. These management strategies will provide FHFA employees with the opportunities, skills, tools, and materials they need in a timely manner to achieve their individual performance goals as well as FHFA's strategic goals.

Careful and collaborative planning will be necessary to ensure that *FHFA's Strategic Plan: Fiscal Years 2015-2019* is supported and that agency resources are available and employed efficiently to support planned activities. FHFA management, technical and program support personnel, and administrative staff will work together to develop long-term workforce, acquisition, and technology plans, as well as logistical plans for space, supplies, and transportation that align with strategic and annual plans.

These plans will be modified as necessary to remain relevant in the face of shifting priorities or unanticipated external events. The plans also will identify the skills, funding, and resources necessary to achieve planned FHFA results and specify the timeframes for acquiring the needed resources. FHFA will continue working to secure the resources needed to fulfill its critical mission and achieve the goals and outcomes outlined in this Strategic Plan.

APPENDIX A: STRATEGIC PLANNING PROCESS

FHFA developed the *FHFA Strategic Plan: Fiscal Years 2015-2019* through an inclusive process within the agency. With guidance from the Director, FHFA managers and other subject matter experts were actively involved with the development of the strategic and performance goals contained in this Strategic Plan.

To monitor FHFA's goal achievement progress, FHFA senior managers will meet quarterly to evaluate performance and to identify obstacles that might prevent the agency from achieving a goal. FHFA will also use regular management meetings, all-hands meetings, management reports, and performance review meetings to communicate and discuss organizational goals and objectives. FHFA employees will align their job performance plans and individual development plans to support FHFA's strategic and performance goals.

APPENDIX B: Consultation and Outreach

FHFA invited input from Congress, stakeholders, and the public on the *FHFA Strategic Plan: Fiscal Years 2015-2019* through a posting on the agency's website over a 30-day period in August 2014. FHFA received 26 comments to the Plan and carefully reviewed each, making changes in the final version where appropriate.

APPENDIX C: Program Evaluations

Program evaluation is an important feedback tool that can provide managers with information to ensure that FHFA's goals are meaningful and the strategies for achieving them effective. The data and information from FHFA's program evaluations enable staff and senior management to assess goal achievement and plan future programs. FHFA considers the findings from these evaluations and audits in order to improve agency operations. The primary internal and external evaluations are listed below.

Internal

Executive Committee on Internal Controls FHFA's Executive Committee on Internal Controls meets quarterly to review the results of internal and external program evaluations. The committee evaluates the findings and establishes appropriate remediation activities for FHFA. Committee activities provide input to FHFA's determinations of the adequacy of internal controls under Office of Management and Budget Circular A-123.

☐ ☐ice o☐☐ ualit☐ ☐ssurance☐ FHFA has established an Office of Quality Assurance as part of the agency's overall internal control structure. The Office of Quality Assurance's primary responsibility is to measure and evaluate the quality of work of FHFA divisions and offices, based on an annual risk assessment and as specific needs are identified.

E☐ternal

☐ ☐ice o☐☐ns☐ector General☐ The Office of Inspector General has a large role in program evaluation. The office reviews various aspects of agency operations to guard against waste, fraud, and abuse. FHFA's Office of Inspector General fills the vital role of ensuring the integrity of FHFA by conducting independent and objective audits, evaluations, and investigations, helping FHFA to achieve its mission and goals.

The Office of Inspector General also annually reviews the agency's information security program through its internal audit function and reports the results to the Office of Management and Budget, as required by the Federal Information Security Management Act. FHFA uses these audits and reviews to implement improvements in its information security program.

Go☐ernment ☐ccountabilit☐ ☐ ☐☐ice☐ The Government Accountability Office, an investigative arm of Congress, audits FHFA's financial statements, periodically conducts targeted reviews of FHFA's programs and initiatives, and testifies before Congress on its observations and recommendations.

Congressional ☐udget ☐ ☐☐ice☐ The Congressional Budget Office, also an arm of Congress, periodically issues reports and analytical studies of issues related to the costs, benefits, and risks of the regulated entities and their oversight and testifies before Congress on its findings.

Office of Personnel Management. The Office of Personnel Management periodically conducts reviews of FHFA human capital operations to ensure they support the agency's human capital management and are in compliance with merit system principles.

Office of Government Ethics. The Office of Government Ethics periodically conducts reviews of the FHFA ethics program to ensure that it meets the requirements set forth by law, regulation, and OGE guidance.

National Archives and Records Administration. The National Archives and Records Administration reviews the annual agency self-assessment submitted by FHFA to ensure that FHFA is in compliance with statutory and regulatory recordkeeping requirements.